*This book was purchased
with funds from a
generous donation by*

Dr. Kathryn W. Davis

GREAT FILMMAKERS
CLINT EASTWOOD

Will Mara

Cavendish
Square
New York

Published in 2015 by Cavendish Square Publishing, LLC,
243 5th Avenue, Suite 136, New York, NY 10016

CPSIA Compliance Information: Batch #WS14CSQ

All websites were available and accurate when this book was sent to press.

Library of Congress Cataloging-in-Publication Data

Mara, Wil.
Clint Eastwood / by Wil Mara.
p. cm. — (Great filmmakers)
Includes index.
ISBN 978-1-62712-948-0 (hardcover) ISBN 978-1-62712-950-3 (ebook)
1. Eastwood, Clint, 1930- — Juvenile literature. 2. Motion picture actors and actresses — United States — Biography — Juvenile literature. 3. Motion picture producers and directors — United States — Biography — Juvenile literature. I. Mara, Wil. II. Title.
PN2287.E37 M36 2015
791.43—d23

Editorial Director: Dean Miller
Editor: Fletcher Doyle
Copy Editor: Cynthia Roby
Art Director: Jeffrey Talbot

Senior Designer: Amy Greenan
Production Manager: Jennifer Ryder-Talbot
Production Editor: David McNamara
Photo Researcher: J8 Media

The photographs in this book are used by permission and through the courtesy of:
Cover and page 1, Bobby Bank/Wirelmage/Getty Images; © celebrity/Alamy, 5; Dorothea Lange (1895-1965)/File:Poor mother and children, Oklahoma, 1936 by Dorothea Lange. jpg/Wikimedia Commons, 7; Photo courtesy of Seth Poppel, 9; Universal Images Group/ Getty Images, 10; Hulton Archive/Archive Photos/Getty Images, 11; pagadesign/E+/Getty Images, 12, 24, 41, 52, 60; www.demilked.com/free-paper-textures-backgrounds, 12–13, 24–25, 41, 52, 60; CBS Photo Archive/Getty Images, 13; Silver Screen Collection/Moviepix/ Getty Images, 15; CBS Photo Archive/Getty Images, 17; © MARKA/Alamy, 19; Silver Screen Collection/Moviepix/Getty Images, 20; MGM Studios/Moviepix/Getty Images, 23; Archive Photos/Moviepix/Getty Images, 25; AP Photo/Paul Sakuma, 29; David Madison/ Getty Images, 32; Bill Eppridge/The LIFE Picture Collection/Getty Images, 35; Silver Screen Collection/Moviepix/Getty Images, 36; Michael Ochs Archives/Moviepix/Getty Images, 40; Michael Ochs Archives/Moviepix/Getty Images, 41; Hulton Archive/Getty Images, 45; © Pictorial Press Ltd/Alamy, 49; © Mark Reinstein/Globe Photos/Zumapress.com, 53; J. Vespa/ Wirelmage/Getty Images, 57; Vera Anderson/Wirelmage/Getty Images, 60; Kevin Winter/ Getty Images, 62.

Printed in the United States of America

GREAT FILMMAKERS
CLINT EASTWOOD

1 HIS OWN MAN

The name Clint Eastwood conjures several images. The most recent of these is the political conservative who famously spoke to an empty chair during a speech in support of candidate Mitt Romney at the Republican National Convention in 2012. Then there is his older film persona, the taciturn gunfighter/policeman who would say in *Pink Cadillac*, "I have a firm policy on gun control. If there's a gun around, I want to be in control of it." There is also the award-winning **director** who brought us surprises such as *The Bridges of Madison County* and *Gran Torino*.

None of this comes close to telling the story of a man who has added a successful directing career to an acting career, who has refused to be wedded to any movie **genre**, who has produced award-winning work at an age when most people have long retired, and who has held political office.

His is the story of a man who became a student

4

Clint Eastwood has always been big, weighing 11 pounds (5 kilograms) at birth.

of his craft, always learning, always searching for new challenges, never afraid to take risks. Interestingly, he did it all after getting into his life's work almost by accident.

Unlike most others in the movie business, it wasn't something that interested him as a youth. His childhood did have a big impact on his film work— as well as on his politics, however.

Clint Eastwood's parents, Clinton and Ruth, met while at Piedmont High School, in Oakland, California. This was in the mid 1920s, not long after World War I, when America's economy was sailing high. They were from working-class stock and were married not long after they finished high school, in June of 1927. Ruth was only eighteen years old.

Clinton Jr., their first child, was born three years later in San Francisco; he weighed more than 11 pounds (5 kg). In October of the previous year, the stock market had crashed, ushering in the Great Depression. It was one of darkest eras in American history, with banks failing, record unemployment, widespread panic, and families disintegrating as men became nomads searching for work.

Seeing this shaped his guiding principles. In a 1982 interview with Barbara Walters, he said: "My dad used to preach to me all the time, 'Nobody's going to give you anything, you'll have to go out and earn whatever you're going to get. That was the philosophy in those days. People went out and earned things. I remember people used to come to the door in those days and ask if they could, instead of asking for a handout, they'd ask if they could work for something. Guys would say, 'Can I chop wood for you' or 'Can I sweep off the driveway or something for a sandwich.' And that was the philosophy. Nowadays we seem to be in more of a 'What can big daddy do for

6

The Great Depression hit many families hard, and taught Clint Eastwood to be self-sufficient.

us, the big daddy government?' ... It seems like people were more individualistic in those days."

In 1934, the Eastwoods had a second child, a daughter named Jeanne. It wasn't long after this that the family began a difficult period of road travel as Clinton searched for work.

Eastwood said of his upbringing: "I moved around a lot. I was born in 1930 and lived in various towns in California, up and down: Sacramento Valley, Los Angeles for a little bit, Oakland, all these areas. But I had good parents who I think did the best they could, so I had a reasonable childhood. It was kind of lonely in some ways because you never went to the same school for six or seven months, you were always moving on somewhere. But it was OK."

The family landed back in Oakland after the start of World War II. When America was pulled into it following the Japanese attack on Pearl Harbor in December of 1941, Eastwood's father found a job in the steel industry, which was booming due to wartime demand. His mother got a job at IBM.

"I'm sure I wasn't the easiest child to raise, especially with both of them working," Eastwood said. "I was like most kids: It's amazing how much smarter your parents get after you turn 21."

With so much bouncing around, young Clint never got the chance to establish himself in any one school system or neighborhood. As a result, he made few friends, developed into something of a loner, and learned to keep most of his thoughts and feelings to himself. This kind of moody silence was to become a key element of many of his on-screen characters.

His mother said in a TV documentary that his upbringing meant that Eastwood often invented imaginary friends, and she thought this was what led to his becoming an actor.

When he did manage to settle into a school for a time, he found it difficult to get interested in the academics. He got involved with sports, following in his father's footsteps: His father had been inducted into the Piedmont High School Football Hall of Fame. He also liked jazz, and took pains to learn to play the piano. Both his athleticism and his musical talent made him popular, and because he was good-looking, slim, and muscular like his father, he had no trouble attracting the attention of women.

Eastwood loved cars, and worked a series of part-time jobs to earn gas and repair money. The work

Clint Eastwood was good-looking and attracted the attention of many girls, but he was still something of a loner.

and his casual interest in academics contributed to a drop in his grades. He was forced to transfer from Piedmont High School to Oakland Technical High School, from which he graduated in early 1949.

Not long afterward, Clint's father was offered a steady managerial position in Seattle. The young Eastwood was tired of moving and felt he was old enough to stay behind in the Oakland area. He lived with a friend's family and worked jobs that provided no real future, all the while indulging in his passions for cars, girls, and music. Then came America's entry into the Korean War. Eastwood—single, young, healthy, and no longer a student—was drafted. In early 1951, he traveled to Fort Ord, located on Monterey Bay in west-central California, to begin his basic training.

California's Fort Ord introduced Clint Eastwood to the Monterey Peninsula.

Getting a Break

Getting drafted during wartime might not seem like a lucky break, but for Eastwood, Fort Ord provided an introduction to three things that became vitally important to him.

When he reported for duty he expected to be trained to be shipped overseas. Instead, he was made a swimming instructor, which meant he'd be spending most of his work time at the base pool. The military had also drafted many actors and actresses and wasn't eager to put any of them on the battlefield. Instead, it made them part of a branch of the military known as "Special Services." It was common for Hollywood stars to make short films, public-service pieces, or ordinary commercials to be used for propaganda that stirred public backing of the war effort. The rest of the time, these stars were free to do as they pleased—and many of them spent their spare time at the Fort Ord pool.

This provided Eastwood with contacts within the film industry, including David Janssen (*The Fugitive*) and Martin Milner (*Route 66*, *Adam-12*). They urged him to go into acting, saying his looks would make him a natural in front of the camera.

Eastwood also gained an appreciation of the spectacular Monterey area, which he made his home as soon as he could afford it. He calls his 2,040-acre property high above Monterey Bay, which he bought in the late 1970s, Tehama.

And the third thing he gained was an introduction to his first wife. During one off-base excursion to visit an old friend at Berkeley, he met Maggie Johnson, who had been a swimsuit model. When Eastwood's army service ended in the summer of 1953, he traveled to Los Angeles, where Maggie was living with her parents following her college graduation. He accepted a series of odd jobs and signed up for business classes in the hope that they

Clint Eastwood has been married twice. His first wife, Maggie Johnson, was a swimsuit model.

BIG DADDY

In spite of Eastwood's affection for Maggie Johnson, his marriage to her would not work out. Maggie put up with his infidelities for as long as she could, but the couple separated in 1978 and formally divorced in 1984. Eastwood would get married just one more time, to twenty-eight-year-old TV journalist Dina Marie Ruiz in 1996, but she filed for divorce late in 2013. He would have two other serious, long-term relationships in the years prior to marrying Ruiz—one with actress and singer Sandra Locke from 1975 to 1989 (Locke would also costar with Eastwood in several films) and another with English actress Frances Fisher from 1990 to 1995. Eastwood has eight children, although only two are the product of either of his marriages.

Eastwood is widely quoted as saying, "They say marriages are made in Heaven. But so is thunder and lightning."

Clint and Maggie tried to make their marriage work, but it ended in divorce in 1984.

Despite what seems to be a somewhat messy family situation stemming from his romantic activities, he does appear to have strong relationships with his children, as well as most of his former partners. Locke was the exception, and she aired their dirty laundry in her memoir, *The Good, the Bad and the Very Ugly*.

might increase his earning power. He also started attending acting classes. Clint and Maggie were married at the end of 1953 and moved into a house in nearby South Oakhurst.

Cast Me, Maybe

In early 1954, Eastwood took a screen test at Universal Studios, which had recently launched a new television department to produce shows that featured tough-guy roles. Eastwood, despite having little in the way of formal training or acting skills, was signed to a contract for seventy-five dollars a week.

With this opportunity finally in front of him, Eastwood decided to get serious about acting. He took more classes and tried to soak up as much as he could.

"We were a bunch of flunkies just hanging around—'Give me a bit here, teach me something...' You'd try to learn as much as you could. I'd go to everybody's sets, just watch people. ... And the advantage of doing a TV series in the late '50s or early '60s was, you'd get to work with different directors, some of whom had done great movies."

His work ethic was instilled by his father, who died at the age of sixty-four. "He believed in hard work," Eastwood said of his father in an interview. "'Nothing comes for nothing,' he'd say. 'You have to work for whatever you get.' When I wanted to go and be an actor and I was gonna drop out of school because seventy-five bucks sounded like a lot to me, he said, 'God, don't do that. Continue your education.' He said, 'Don't get in this dreamworld...'"

Acting attracted him a lot more than taking business classes, and by mid-1954, Universal felt Eastwood was ready for some on-screen roles.

One of Clint Eastwood's early roles was in 1955's *Revenge of the Creature*—the sequel to the popular *Creature from the Black Lagoon*.

His first was as a laboratory worker in the "B" movie *Revenge of the Creature*. Released in May of 1955, it was the first sequel to the hugely popular horror flick *Creature from the Black Lagoon*. He was in just one scene and had only a few lines. Further, his name did not appear in the credits.

After a year and a half, Universal let him go. He went through an agonizing period of modulating between ho-hum acting jobs and the occasional laborer's job. He continued to get tiny parts in feature films, most of which were still uncredited, plus a few television roles, such as his appearance as a character named John Lucas in two episodes of the popular series *Death Valley Days*. But none of these opportunities provided him with much more than a small paycheck.

2 LAUNCHING A CAREER

In the late 1950s, westerns were the most popular shows on television. The CBS network was enjoying tremendous success with *Gunsmoke*. To capitalize on this popularity it developed a similar show it named *Rawhide*. It was set after the Civil War, as was *Gunsmoke*, and followed two cattlemen and their crew as they drove a large herd across the American plains.

For the lead role, CBS cast Eric Fleming as trail boss Gil Favor. Fleming had done some stage work in Chicago and New York as well as a few minor television roles and "B" films. For Gil Favor's sidekick, Rowdy Yates, CBS wanted someone just as handsome but younger. They also wanted someone who could convey toughness and sensitivity. After meeting hundreds of people, *Rawhide* **producer** Robert Sparks sized up Clint Eastwood and liked the look of him. The first words Sparks spoke to Eastwood weren't "Hello" or "How are you doing?" but rather "How tall are you?"—and he had the six-foot-four (1.93 m) actor come in for a screen test

Clint Eastwood's first big role was on the hit show *Rawhide*.

the next day. A week later Eastwood got word that he had been given the part.

Rawhide was so popular that 217 episodes were produced, spanning eight seasons. It spent most of that time in a prime Friday slot, switching to Tuesdays only toward the end of its run. The writers weren't afraid to address topics more substantial than those usually found in westerns, such as morphine use and racism, giving *Rawhide* credibility as more than just a "shoot 'em up" program. Fleming left the show before its final season, and Eastwood's character became the new trail boss and the star of the program.

During *Rawhide*'s successful run, Eastwood's salary reached $100,000 a year. But as his popularity increased, so did the demands on his time. A private person by nature, he disliked the constant attention from the public. And as the series reached its later seasons, he found the daily grind of the shooting schedule (sometimes six, even seven days a week) exhausting. He became restless and soon identified what lay at the core of it—he needed a fresh challenge.

"In *Rawhide* I did get awfully tired of playing the conventional white hat. The hero who kisses old ladies and dogs and was kind to everybody. I decided it was time to be an anti-hero."

He got that chance when he went to work with Sergio Leone, an Italian director, producer, and **screenwriter**. In the early 1960s, he was a key player in the creation of a new film genre known as the spaghetti western. It embraced the spirit of the American western but was shot in Europe, usually in Spain or Italy, and often with multilingual casts and overdubs.

Leone injected his spaghetti westerns with a sense of moral ambiguity among his characters that

Director Sergio Leone played a huge role
in launching Clint Eastwood's movie career
by casting him in a trio of popular
spaghetti westerns.

Eastwood would import into many of his own future
films. In a Leone western, clear lines were not always
drawn between the "good guys" and the "bad guys."

In American westerns, the good guys were
exemplars of human goodness, uncompromising
in their principles and unswerving supporters of
morals and values. They were idealized role models
for youngsters. In a Leone western, the hero might
be unshaven, rude, indifferent, even callous.
Underlying this rough veneer, he would still have
that unshakable sense of right and wrong—but he
wasn't the type of man you'd necessarily want your
children to emulate. Eastwood would play these
anti-hero protagonists with great success.

The first collaboration between Leone and
Eastwood was *A Fistful of Dollars*. The main character

Eastwood's 'Stranger' character in the Sergio Leone films set the tone for many of the tough-guy roles he would later play.

was a mysterious figure known as "the Stranger," who wandered into the fictional town of San Miguel, which sat on the border of the United States and Mexico. At the time of the Stranger's arrival, two factions are battling for control of San Miguel—the Baxters, led by sheriff John Baxter, and the Rojos, three brothers known for their brutality. Neither side knows what to make of the Stranger, who gives away little of himself but is a master at gunplay.

Leone said it didn't take long for him to realize Eastwood was perfect for this new breed of gunfighter. "At that time I needed a mask rather than an actor, and Eastwood had only two facial expressions: one with the hat and one without it."

Eastwood saw it as a way to expand his acting repertoire, and felt his silence added to the mystery of the character and allowed him to grow in the imagination of the audience. He played the Stranger with a kind of steely indifference that is intriguing and unsettling.

This apparent lack of emotion, of keeping one's feelings hidden, fits in with Eastwood the person. "There are certain things I just don't enjoy sharing with everybody else. There's certain thoughts that I don't feel compelled to, to tell every thought that's in my mind," he said.

And when asked if this reserve even applied to the women in his life, he answered, "[I] only talk about certain things but there's never a 100 percent. If you break it down into 100 percent, you might talk 60 percent. A woman would go absolutely nuts if she knew 100 percent about a person. She might be bored because there's nothing left to know. Somebody who's that interested, I'd wonder why she was that interested. Why aren't they enjoying the fact that there's more to know all the time?"

A Fistful of Dollars hit theaters in Italy in the fall of 1964 and became the highest-grossing film there of all time. When it reached the United States in January 1967 (CBS didn't want the movie shown while Eastwood was still on *Rawhide*) it grossed just over $14 million, which was remarkable when one considers that the film's budget was only around $200,000. Out of that, Eastwood was paid $15,000.

Leone made two other spaghetti westerns with Eastwood, creating what is known as the Dollars Trilogy. They were filmed over the summer when shooting for *Rawhide* was on hiatus. The others were *For a Few Dollars More*, for which Eastwood received $50,000, and *The Good, the Bad, and the Ugly*, for which he received $250,000 as well as a percentage of ticket sales. Both were financially successful.

One aspect of filmmaking that set Leone apart was he was more interested in the moments that led up to the actions than in drawing out long action sequences. In the climactic gunfight at the end of *The Good, the Bad, and the Ugly*, tension builds as Leone provides repeated close-ups of the protagonists before any of them dies. There is only one shot fired.

Eastwood and Leone would not work together again. Leone was a demanding director with a sometimes flashpoint temper, and while the young actor was willing to deal with it at the beginning of their collaboration, by the end of *The Good, the Bad, and the Ugly* he had grown weary of it. When Leone offered him the lead role in his next film, *Once Upon a Time in the West*, Eastwood passed.

"Sergio was terrific for me," Eastwood said in an interview. "I was this young man, having done three years on *Rawhide*, with an Italian director who spoke no English. I thought it was insanity and that insanity was intriguing for me."

Eastwood Gets Dirty

As the '60s eased into the '70s, Eastwood continued accepting the tough-guy roles that were becoming his trademark. He still did a fair share of films with western settings. Some of the more memorable of these include 1968's *Hang 'Em High*, 1969's *Paint Your Wagon*, and 1970's *Two Mules for Sister Sara* alongside Shirley MacLaine. *Hang 'Em High* was the most successful, but Eastwood was growing weary of cowboy roles and wanted a new vehicle for his talents.

In 1970, Eastwood starred alongside Donald Sutherland (left) and Don Rickles in the military comedy *Kelly's Heroes*.

He did a few films with a military theme. The first was 1968's action-packed *Where Eagles Dare*, which involved a mission behind Nazi lines and which featured an all-star cast that included Richard Burton. The second was 1970's *Kelly's Heroes*. The movie was primarily a comedy, a genre with which Eastwood had little experience. For support, he was surrounded by a cast that included Telly Savalas (*Kojak*), Don Rickles (*CPO Sharkey*), Carroll O'Connor (*All in the Family*), Donald Sutherland (*The Dirty Dozen*), and Gavin McLeod (*The Love Boat*).

He got back on more familiar turf with his portrayals of policemen. His first significant film in this

WIT AND WISDOM

Among Eastwood's numerous contributions to film and television, one of the most impressive has to be the list of unforgettable lines his characters have delivered—bits of dialogue that have since woven their way into the fabric of American culture. Here are some of his most famous:

"Go ahead, make my day."
—*Sudden Impact*

"A man's got to know his limitations."
—*Magnum Force*

"Dyin' ain't much of a livin', boy."
—*The Outlaw Josey Wales*

"You see, in this world there's two kinds of people, my friend: Those with loaded guns, and those who dig. You dig."
—*The Good, the Bad, and the Ugly*

"If you want a guarantee, buy a toaster."
—*The Rookie*

Clint Eastwood hit box-office gold with his 'Dirty Harry' character.

"I know what you're thinking. 'Did he fire six shots or only five?' Well, to tell you the truth, in all this excitement I kind of lost track myself. But being as this is a .44 Magnum, the most powerful handgun in the world, and would blow your head clean off, you've got to ask yourself one question: Do I feel lucky? Well, do ya, punk?"
—*Dirty Harry*

"Well, if you're waitin' for a woman to make up her mind, you may have a long wait."
—*Pale Rider*

regard was 1968's *Coogan's Bluff*, his first with another of his mentors, director Don Siegel. His character, Walt Coogan, doesn't get along with his boss because he's opinionated and doesn't always do things by the book. His boss sends him from Arizona to New York to collect a prisoner for transfer and, disgusted by all the bureaucracy surrounding his prisoner's release, he gets the prisoner out by breaking a few rules. When the prisoner escapes, Coogan's boss is delighted with his failure and orders him to return home to face punishment. Coogan defies these orders and sets out in search of the prisoner.

Eastwood began to identify with this "man against the system" character, and it is a part of who he is. "To some people I represent a dying individuality within our system," he said in a 1982 interview with Barbara Walters. "I feel there is a crying out for individuals. I feel that because of the intellect of the human race, we've bogged ourselves down in such bureaucratic nonsense that it seems like we've made life much more complicated than it should be. I guess I'm for the system but I'm against the inequities of the system."

Coogan's Bluff didn't do particularly well in theaters, but it set the tone for another, similar character that Eastwood would turn into a worldwide sensation. A few years later, he began work on a film with Siegel called *Dirty Harry*, which followed the struggles of embittered cop Harry Callahan as he tries to get things done in the political world of the San Francisco Police Department.

"You kind of have a hunch," Eastwood said about the character who would define his career. "There was a loneliness about the guy, he had an empty life, but he also had this obsession with getting criminals off the street."

In this first story, the town of San Francisco is caught in the grip of a lunatic sniper called Scorpio, who is randomly killing citizens until the city gives in to his demands for money. Harry Callahan, nicknamed "Dirty Harry" because he plays as dirty as he feels is necessary to do his job, is assigned to stop Scorpio. Harry does, only to watch in frustration as the killer is set free because the manner of his arrest violated strict department rules. It isn't long before Scorpio goes after more innocent victims—a busload of children—and San Francisco's mayor decides to give in to his demands. But Dirty Harry, fed up and more determined than ever, has other ideas.

"Being a contrary sort of person, I figured there had been enough politically correct crap going around. The police were not held in great favor particularly, the Miranda decisions had come down [forcing police to read arrested suspects their rights], people were thinking about the plight of the accused. I thought, 'Let's do a picture about the plight of the victim.'"

Dirty Harry, released in December of 1971, was a massive hit, earning more than $35 million at the **box office** from a production budget of less than $4 million. The story laid bare the unpleasant truth that overwrought systems and establishments can often defeat their own reason for being, that a police department can get so tangled in regulations that it is forced to let a killer go free. A man like Harry Callahan, willing to blow off such rigid structure in the interest of just getting things done, appealed to millions of viewers—and it wasn't long before they were demanding that Dirty Harry return to the big screen.

3 HOME BY THE BAY

The beautiful town of Carmel-by-the-Sea, California, has been Eastwood's home since the late 1970s. "I bought it I can't even tell you how long ago—over 30 years," he said of his land in a 2007 interview. "I was drafted in the Army in 1951 and was stationed at Fort Ord. I always liked Carmel. I thought if I ever could afford to, or figure out how to make a living there, I might like to live there."

His home is on 2,040 acres of rolling hills and canyons that are populated by deer, fox, turkey, quail, and lots of other wildlife. The setting is perfect for a man who remains intensely private despite his fame.

"People like me are looking for a place where they can have a quiet life and yet still be close to things. Me? I like elbow room. But it's nice to know that if I want to go to the Carmel Bach Festival, or listen to some jazz in Monterey, or watch the

Voters chose
Clint Eastwood
as mayor of
Carmel-by-the-Sea,
California.

Concours d'Elegance in Pebble Beach, it's just minutes away. If you want to go to dinner in Carmel or Monterey, you don't have to drive forever to get home," he said.

The land also provides him a place where he can find peace from his high-pressure career.

"I'm not always calm. And though I'm fairly in control most of the time I can be very uncalm," he said. "…You do pay for that. Sometimes, people who get things off their chest get a certain relief from that. It's like going out in the middle of the highway and yelling obscenities, there is some release to that. You can come back and say 'wow'."

People also release tension by talking through their problems, another tactic Eastwood dismisses. "I know a lot of people get a release from that. That's why psychiatrists make so much money, because you can sit down and really unload, but to me I've never felt that. I don't particularly want to unload on anybody else … I always felt I could go out and walk through this field (in Carmel) and look at these flowers and these trees and unload by myself."

Move into Politics

Carmel has a population of fewer than four thousand people, most of them affluent and involved in the artistic world. Some of Eastwood's neighbors include author Beverly Cleary, comedian Craig Kilborn, and legendary actress Doris Day.

Eastwood loved the town so deeply that he wanted to take part in its day-to-day affairs. He ran for, and won with 72.5 percent of the vote, the office of mayor, serving from 1986 to 1988. He did this with no particular political affiliation, for although his image suggests to many a strong conservative streak, he is in fact a **libertarian**. In 2004, he made this position quite clear when he told *USA Weekend*, "I don't see myself as conservative, but I'm not ultra-leftist. You build a philosophy of your own. I like the libertarian view, which is to leave everyone alone. Even as a kid, I was annoyed by people who wanted to tell everyone how to live."

He felt no compulsion to give up making movies for a career in politics. "I enjoyed being mayor of Carmel but you do see that it is very difficult to get things done," he said in an interview. "You just have to lose your soul. You have to BS people. You have to deal with people you don't care for and will never be friends with, so you kind of sell yourself out to be a politician. You have to kiss it up with the world. That ain't my style."

Even after his time in office, Eastwood continued to actively support the Carmel community, taking positions on issues such as business growth, road construction, and environmental conservation.

He also has kept many family members nearby. His mother, who died in February 2006 at the age of ninety-seven, lived the last sixteen years of her life at Hacienda Carmel, close to the golf course at Tehama. His sister also lives in the Carmel Valley, as did actress Frances Fisher and their actress daughter, Francesca.

Eastwood stayed close to his mother, even after she remarried following the death of his father in 1970. "She just wanted me to do my best at whatever it was," said Eastwood, whose strong work ethic is part of his Hollywood reputation. "In my family, we were taught it wasn't a sin to work and that it was important to contribute."

Clint Eastwood has long held a passion for golf.

Ruth Wood was a fan of her son's work, telling the *San Francisco Chronicle* that when one of her son's movies came out, she "was the first one in the theater every time."

Eastwood's Carmel property allows him to stay in great shape—he takes long walks on the wild beaches and in the wooded hills—and it lets him pursue his passion for golf.

He has kept most of his property in a natural state with the exception of building the Tehama Golf Club, which requires an invitation to join. However, he did develop it with an eye toward ecology. "We did it all with native grasses. The only thing we seeded was the greens," he said. "The late John Zoller was our guy. He got us experimenting with native grasses … We didn't cut a lot of trees. We moved a few around: 200- and 300-year-old oaks. Slid them 25 yards over. The trees are very healthy up there. Much younger."

He has sponsored a charity tournament at Tehama since the early 2000s and has been a long-time participant in the Pebble Beach National Pro-Am. In an incident at a dinner for volunteers on the night before the tournament in February 2014, he showed how vital he still is. "Clint saved my life," tournament director Steve John told the *Carmel Pine Cone*. "We were just talking. A piece of cheese went in my mouth and suddenly I couldn't breathe. It was as bad as it could have been. Clint came up behind me and he knew exactly what to do. He did the Heimlich maneuver and he lifted me right off the ground. He's strong! The cheese popped out and I was fine."

"I looked in his eyes and saw that look of panic people have when they see their life passing before their eyes," Eastwood told the *Carmel Pine Cone*. "It looked bad … I gave him three good jolts and that got it out. And then I made him drink a big glass of water with a bunch of lemon squeezed in it."

4 IN THE DIRECTOR'S CHAIR

Clint Eastwood, as a film director, is known for several characteristics that can be traced to his growing up during the Depression and the early years of his acting career.

Waste was not an option for almost everyone in the 1930s, and this lesson was not lost on Eastwood. It was reinforced when he worked on *Rawhide*— weekly television series are shot on tight deadlines that must be met, so there is no time to waste.

From Leone he would learn an economical shooting style, which reduced production costs, and the use of close-ups and landscape, which he would incorporate into his own films. From Don Siegel he would learn how to organize and plan a shooting schedule, which leads to efficiency.

Eastwood has been quoted as saying he likes to work efficiently because at the end of the day he likes to feel he's gotten something done. Also, he's not a perfectionist who takes himself too seriously.

Don Siegel confers with
Clint Eastwood on the set
of *Dirty Harry*.

Clint Eastwood made his directorial debut
and starred in *Play Misty for Me*, along with
Donna Mills.

He related an encounter with a very old Alfred
Hitchcock in which "we got to intellectualizing our
movies, and he said, 'You must remember one
thing—it's only a movie.' I said, 'You're right. It won't
cure cancer or any other disease in the world but it
might make somebody happy somewhere.' He said,
'Yeah, that's about it.'"

He also has a reputation for telling stories, as
opposed to making technological marvels, and for
picking subjects of interest to him.

In 1971, at the age of forty-one, Eastwood found
success with the first *Dirty Harry* film, and decided to
make his debut as a director. *Play Misty for Me* told

the unsettling story of woman who stalks Eastwood's character, radio DJ Dave Garver, and then goes berserk when Garver rejects her after what he thought was a one-night stand. Although she is committed to a mental hospital, she is soon on the loose, and when she attacks Garver's girlfriend in her apartment and then takes her hostage, Garver has to think fast if he has any hope of saving his girlfriend.

On the movie's appeal, he said that, "At sometime in everyone's life, regardless of the situation they are in, they have had some kind of uncomfortable relationship like that. Where one person interprets a relationship one way and the other person doesn't see it that way."

Play Misty for Me, with a budget of less than a million dollars, earned more than $10 million. Jessica Walter was even nominated for a Golden Globe Award for Best Actress for her chilling portrayal of the unbalanced stalker Evelyn Draper.

"It was always at the back of my mind there was going to come a day when I would direct," said Eastwood. "But it came simply. I did one picture, then I needed to do a western picture because that's the genre I was brought up in so I did (*High Plains Drifter*). Then one thing led to another and … I'm still doing it."

In *High Plains Drifter* he returned to the role of the nameless wanderer he played in the three spaghetti westerns that he did with Sergio Leone. Released in 1973, it earned more than $15 million on a budget of just over $5 million. In an unforgettable homage to his old friend and mentor, Eastwood made sure that one of the headstones that appears in the final scene bears the name "Sergio Leone."

The studio that distributed the film, Universal, was particularly pleased that Eastwood finished all production work a few days ahead of schedule and even under budget. This again was a reflection of his upbringing.

"It seemed like in those days, you had what you had and nothing more," he said of his childhood. "In other words, if you had ten dollars, you had ten dollars. You didn't have one thousand dollars on a credit card that you could just ring up. Nowadays we live in a dream world that offers you something for nothing."

More unusual was the fact that Eastwood shot the film in chronological sequence, as opposed to doing scenes in non-sequential order and then **editing** them together. With this kind of preparation and efficiency, which Eastwood said he learned from Siegel, studios were much more likely to allow him future directing opportunities. He did, in fact, direct three more films in the 1970s. The third, 1976's *The Outlaw Josey Wales*, struck gold. Eastwood played the lead role of Josey Wales, a peaceful farmer, husband, and father whose wife and children are murdered by a band of lawless Jayhawkers— pro-Union guerrillas—at the end of the Civil War.

The Outlaw Josey Wales turned out to be a hit with both moviegoers and critics, earning more than $30 million on a budget of less than $4 million and receiving excellent reviews. Particularly impressive was Eastwood's part as a wronged man fighting for justice in a postwar America marred by lawlessness and lingering tension. The film did receive one **Academy Award** nomination (for Original Music **Score**), and in 1996 it became the first of three associated with him to be entered into the National Film Preservation Board of the Library of Congress' National Film Registry. The others were *Unforgiven* (2004) and *Dirty Harry* (2012).

New Horizons

The biggest departure by Eastwood from his tough-guy image came in 1978, when he again stepped into the world of comedy with *Every Which Way but Loose*. He played a California truck driver with the unlikely name of Philo Beddoe, who lives in a little suburban house with his scatterbrained mother and an orangutan named Clyde. His best friend, Orville, lives in the house behind them. Philo is partial to wearing jeans, boots, and tight white T-shirts that emphasize his physique, and his strength is such that he makes extra money by traveling to bare-fisted boxing matches, which are illegal, but which he always wins.

During the course of the story, Philo falls in love with a nightclub singer named Lynn Halsey-Taylor, who then disappears. He and Orville (and Clyde, of course) hit the road in search of her. Along the way, Orville also falls in love (with a girl named Echo), Philo enrages a group of lunatic bikers, and gets into one more fight—with the man rumored to be the greatest brawler of them all.

Every Which Way but Loose went against the way Eastwood was typecast and it showed his independent streak. "People are submitting you a lot of stuff, but you're still trying to do things that are interesting to you and that you think will be interesting to the audience. And then some people think you're crazy. Every advisor I had said, 'Don't do the orangutan movie. Don't do *Every Which Way but Loose*. You can't do this. This is not you.' I said, 'Nothing's me. I'm just plain.'"

Most critics hated the movie. Janet Maslin of the *New York Times* wrote, "The bright new star of

Some critics felt the star of Clint Eastwood's 1978 comedy *Every Which Way but Loose* was Clyde the orangutan.

Every Which Way but Loose is an orangutan named Clyde ... Clyde's many talents notwithstanding, it's alarming to find Clint Eastwood costarring with an ape." In spite of the critical pans, the film earned more money at the box office than almost any other film that year, more than $100 million. That's an incredible achievement in light of the fact that Warner Brothers, which distributed it, wanted to pass on the **script** before Eastwood talked them out of it. It also become one of the most profitable films of Eastwood's entire career—and proof, once and for all, that he was just as capable of delivering a laugh as he was a knockout punch or a gunshot wound. *Every Which Way but Loose* was also a landmark film for Eastwood in that it was his first as a producer. A producer is the top "manager" of a film and can be responsible for everything from getting the

THE NEXT GENERATION

Honkytonk Man was a significant film in the Eastwood canon in that the central character, young Whit, is played by Eastwood's son, Kyle. Artistic talent, it appears, runs strong through Eastwood's bloodlines.

Kyle, his son with his first wife, Maggie, is a professional jazz musician. His daughter Alison, also from that marriage, is an actress, director, model, and fashion designer.

His daughter Francesca, from his relationship with English actress Frances Fisher, is also an actress and model, and his son Scott, from a relationship Eastwood had with flight attendant Jacelyn Allen Reeves, also acts and models.

necessary funding to hiring directors, actors, and crew and finding and developing storylines.

In true Hollywood tradition, Warner Brothers was eager to get Eastwood into a sequel as soon as possible. In the summer of 1980, he began work on *Any Which Way You Can*. Most of the characters from the first film returned, including Clyde the Orangutan, but it was not as successful as the original.

A Breakout Role

In late 1978, Eastwood took on an unusual role simply because it interested him. That role would be of Frank Morris, inmate of the notorious Alcatraz prison, located on San Francisco's Alcatraz Island. The film, titled *Escape from Alcatraz*, tells of Morris's incarceration, his early prison experiences—which include fending off thugs as well as making a few friends—and his attempt with three other inmates to break out of the prison from which no one had ever escaped. The script had been put together by an amateur writer, who'd had no luck getting agents or producers interested in it. He then lied about a previous meeting he'd had with director Don Siegel in order to get Siegel to read it. Siegel liked it and passed it to Eastwood. The two men shot the film on-site, which was no longer being used as a prison. The movie pulled in well over $40 million from a budget of just $8 million. The storyline was intriguing, sparking a renewed interest not just in Alcatraz itself but also in the fate of the escapees, who were never seen again.

Throughout the '80s, Eastwood would continue casting himself in stories that were a step away from those he'd done before. One such film was *Bronco*

Billy. He plays a cowboy in a very unusual situation—he's the star of a dying Wild West show, and when he moves the show to another town in order to attract a new wave of customers, he meets an angry woman whose new husband has taken all of her money and disappeared. The woman, Miss Lily, has to work for Bronco Billy in order to survive. The two develop feelings for each other in spite of the protests of many of the show's other performers.

In 1982, he began work on a Depression-era piece called *Honkytonk Man*. It tells the tale of a gifted singer named Red Stovall whose dream is to play at the Grand Ole Opry in Nashville, Tennessee. However, Red is suffering from an advanced case of tuberculosis, which interferes with, and ultimately ruins, his audition. Nevertheless, he receives a chance to record some songs in a studio, where he manages to get a few tracks down before finally succumbing to the disease.

In 1989, Eastwood went for originality again, acting in the comedy *Pink Cadillac*. It was a rare film for Eastwood in that it bombed in every way possible. It lost money, and the critics absolutely hated it, commenting on the dimwitted storyline, uninspired action scenes, and unenergetic plot.

As Tough as Ever

In spite of his desire to put himself in unconventional roles during the '70s and '80s, Eastwood was still willing to step back into his macho persona. These types of parts had carried him to stardom, and he knew it would be foolish to abandon them.

The *Dirty Harry* character had been so successful that Eastwood would return to it four more times, in

Magnum Force, *The Enforcer*, *Sudden Impact*, and *The Dead Pool*, which is notable for having a small part played by a very young Jim Carrey, who would later go on to movie superstardom beginning with his *Ace Ventura* films.

By the time of *The Dead Pool*'s release, Eastwood was closing in on sixty years of age, and he felt that he would look unconvincing in the character if he played it again.

A Novel Approach

Even as a reluctant student in his youth, Eastwood always had a busy and curious mind. As he matured, he became an ardent fan of the printed word—books, magazines, newspapers, etc. And like so many other filmmakers in Hollywood, he realized that a successful book made ideal movie fodder, if for no other reason than the fan base was already there.

In the fall of 1994, Eastwood began work on a role that few expected from him—that of the romantic leading man. While he had had love interests in many of his past films, this was the first movie in which he starred that could be classified as a romance. The film was based on the 1993 blockbuster novel *The Bridges of Madison County*. Written by Iowa economics professor and part-time author Robert James Waller, *Madison County* told the story of Robert Kincaid, a professional photographer and loner who travels the world in search of beauty, and Francesca Johnson, an Iowa farm wife who leads a pleasant and secure but mostly boring life. While Kincaid is on assignment for *National Geographic* in Iowa to photograph the covered bridges of Madison County, he stops at

In *The Bridges of Madison County,*
Clint Eastwood played a romantic role
alongside Oscar winner Meryl Streep.

Francesca's farm to ask for directions. Francesca is
alone because her husband and two young children
are away on a trip. The chemistry between Robert
and Francesca is very powerful right from the start,
but their journey toward each other is slow because
their moral sensibilities are holding them back.
They are unable to remain apart and begin a brief
but intense love affair.

Much of the moviegoing public as well as film critics were skeptical of Eastwood's ability to pull off a role of such delicate sensitivity—but he proved them wrong with a strong performance. Eastwood also directed the movie. It helped that his costar was Meryl Streep, one of the most honored actresses in film history. Eastwood impressed studio executives with his remarkable filmmaking efficiency, staying under his $22 million budget and beating the shooting schedule by an incredible ten days. *Bridges* earned nearly $200 million at the box office. The late Gene Siskel, veteran film critic from the *Chicago Tribune*, said at the time, "Eastwood's *Bridges* has the energy and spontaneity of a picture that was shot quickly. And that serves the material well, because it removes the solemnity that could stifle a modern classic."

Two years later, Eastwood found another book that intrigued him enough to bring it to the big screen. *Absolute Power* was the 1996 debut novel of then-attorney David Baldacci, and it grew to be one of that year's best-selling thrillers. In the film, master thief Luther Whitney—played by Eastwood—is in the process of robbing the home of a multimillionaire when the man's wife comes home unexpectedly—with another man—and begins to engage in a little "rough romance." The man accidentally strangles the woman to death—and Whitney, who has witnessed all of this, is stunned to see that the man who just committed this murder is the president of the United States. The president's Secret Service detail arrives along with his chief of staff, and they break many laws by trying to cover up his crime. Soon they learn that there was a witness, and the two Secret Service agents go out to hunt down and silence Luther Whitney.

Eastwood's film version of *Absolute Power*, released in February 1997, received a lukewarm reception from both the public and the critics. There were significant differences between the book and the movie, with many of the changes being ordered by Eastwood. Thus, many fans of the book were disappointed.

He got a similar reaction to his third attempt to turn a successful book, the bestselling *Midnight in the Garden of Good and Evil*, into a successful film. The book, written by John Berendt, tells the gothic tale of a murder trial in Savannah, Georgia. Eastwood, who produced and directed the film, once again asked that significant changes be made to the script, changing the story and removing some of the more colorful characters. Fans of the book were incensed, and early reviews were less than flattering; the movie lost about $5 million.

Never one to give up easily, Eastwood again turned to a novel to direct *True Crime*, the 1997 book by veteran author Andrew Klavan. In Eastwood's 1999 film version, journalist Steve Everett (Eastwood) is researching and writing about the forthcoming death-row execution of Frank Beechum, who was convicted of committing murder during a robbery. Everett finds evidence that leads him to believe Beechum is innocent, and he goes about trying to put all the pieces together before Beechum's execution is carried out.

The film was also marred by lackluster performances and a tepid directing job by Eastwood himself. Critics roasted it, and the public quickly lost interest, forcing it out of theaters weeks earlier than planned. As a result of all these handicaps, the movie became one of the biggest flops of Eastwood's career, earning a meager $16.5 million from a budget of more than $55 million.

5 BETTER WITH AGE

In the summer of 1991, Eastwood picked up a project that he'd kept on the shelf for many years— *Unforgiven*. He didn't want to rush into it because he was all but certain it would be his final western. He plays the role of Will Munny, a retired gunfighter who no longer believes in killing. A widowed father of two who is failing as a hog farmer, he hears of a band of cowboys who attacked a helpless prostitute and goes after a reward offered for their capture. Along for the journey are close friend Ned Logan (Morgan Freeman), also a retired gunslinger, and the "Schofield Kid" (Jaimz Woolvett), who dreams of being a gunfighter like Munny once was. Munny and Logan both try to make the Schofield Kid understand the horrors of killing, no matter how justified the reasons might be. However, the Kid does not truly understand until he shoots one of the cowboys to death and becomes overwhelmed with regret. When Logan is captured, tortured, and also killed, Munny knows he has to turn to his pistols one last time in order to make everything right.

Clint Eastwood starred as a
retired gunfighter in 1991's
Unforgiven. It would be his
last role in a western.

Unforgiven was released in August 1992. It brought in more than any other Eastwood film during its first week of release and eventually spent three straight weeks as the number-one film in North America. It was shot on a budget of just under $15 million and went on to gross nearly $160 million in ticket sales. The reaction on the critics' front was no less enthusiastic, with many calling it one of the best westerns of recent decades and the perfect ending to Eastwood's time in the genre. It was then honored throughout the film industry with an incredible thirteen **Oscar** nominations, of which it won four—including Best Picture and Best Director. It was also recognized by the American Film Institute as one of the best westerns in movie history.

The movie is more than just another western to Eastwood, who has worked hard to avoid repeating what's been done. When asked in a 2011 interview what would make him throw aside a script, he answered: "Repetition. When you become a matinee idol ... you get offered a lot of the same stuff that you were successful with before. I've watched that happen for almost 60 years now. The only way to beat the fad is by going against it. On the other hand, I never wanted to do a western again, and then *Unforgiven* came along. And I've never done one since, because I haven't found [a script] that took the western in a new direction."

You're Never Too Old

In the year following the towering success of *Unforgiven*, Eastwood made a film that again cast him in a distinctly tough-guy kind of role, but with the additional element of addressing the fact that he wasn't young anymore. *In the Line of Fire* had him playing the part of Frank Horrigan, a Secret Service agent who still has a passion for the job but whose age is affecting his ability to perform at the top of his game. He is also haunted by a misstep in his professional past—he was one of the men assigned to protect President John F. Kennedy when Kennedy was assassinated in Dallas in November 1963. Unable to resolve the question of whether he could have saved the president if he had reacted more swiftly, Horrigan turns to alcohol to quiet his demons. In spite of both his haunted past and his advancing years, Horrigan insists on being put on presidential detail because he believes there is a psychopathic killer on the loose (a former government hitman) who plans to kill the present-day president, and Horrigan wants the chance to redeem himself. There is also a subplot involving Horrigan and a beautiful female agent who is torn between her loyalty to the service (which requires her to work "against" Horrigan from time to time) and her growing feelings for him.

In the Line of Fire was filmed mostly in and around the Washington, D.C., area and features some interesting digital effects, including shots of President Kennedy's actual assassination with Eastwood's character added by computer. When it reached theaters in July of 1993, it was an instant hit. It was a fairly expensive film by Eastwood's standards, with a budget of about $40 million. It easily earned that back, and eventually brought in more than $185 million in ticket sales. Critics praised it for being not just a tightly plotted and briskly paced thriller, but also an intelligent one, unlike so many of the mindless, one-action-scene-after-another suspense flicks that were coming into vogue

GOIN' DOWN TO... MALPASO?!

In 1967, Eastwood's financial adviser, Irving Leonard, set up a production company in Eastwood's name called Malpaso Productions. The money from Eastwood's films would then flow through Malpaso rather than directly to him, which would be beneficial for taxation and other reasons. The word *malpaso* is Spanish for "bad step," referring playfully to the advice one of Eastwood's agents gave him when he began acting in the trilogy of Sergio Leone westerns—he'd said it would be a "bad step" in his career. Since the company's inception, it has acted as the production vehicle, in whole or in part, for every movie Eastwood has made. Malpaso Productions is headquartered in Burbank, California.

John Malkovich
was creepy
in his role as
Mitch Leary
opposite Clint
Eastwood in
1993's *In the
Line of Fire*.

at the time. Particularly impressive was veteran
actor John Malkovich's unnerving performance
of psychopathic killer Mitch Leary, which earned
Malkovich an Oscar nomination for Best Supporting
Actor. His was one of three Oscar nominations given
to the film.

Eastwood turned seventy at the start of the new
millennium, an age when many people have long
retired to their easy chair. But Eastwood had no
intention of quitting, especially when there were still
great stories to tell.

"I started out in genres of films—the westerns
and the detectives. I was looking for different stories
that go along with the natural maturing of the years.
I probably would have retired years ago if I hadn't
found interesting things to do," he said in an interview.

Spacing Out

Eastwood's first film of the twenty-first century was a drama called *Space Cowboys*. Once again, he was one of the stars as well as the director and producer. He played Frank Corvin, a retired test pilot who is asked to go into space along with his former crew to fix a Soviet satellite that seems to be malfunctioning and could pose dangers on Earth. Once they get there, Frank discovers that they haven't been told the full truth of the mission, and he and his crew find themselves at the center of a potentially explosive geopolitical situation.

Surrounded by some first-rate supporting actors (Tommy Lee Jones, Donald Sutherland, and James Garner), Eastwood managed to produce *Space Cowboys* in just three months. Exterior shots were made on **location** in American space centers (Kennedy, Johnson, Cape Canaveral), whereas the interiors were done on **soundstages**. The film earned decent reviews and enjoyed modest success at the box office, bringing in over $125 million on a budget of just under half that.

If at First You Don't Succeed

His next two films had him once again trying to turn successful books into hit movies—and again, the results were mixed. The first one, 2002's *Blood Work*, was based on a novel by best-selling author Michael Connelly. The premise was intriguing—an FBI agent who had received a heart transplant is asked to track down the killer of the murder victim whose heart he received. Once more directing, producing, and starring, Eastwood plays the FBI agent in question, Terry McCaleb, and his supporting cast included Anjelica Huston and Jeff Daniels. The shoot took less than two months, and he stuck to a budget of just $50 million. Neither the critics nor the public warmed to his version of the story, and the film lost a lot of money.

Playing the roles of producer, director and lead actor removes some of the checks that can keep a bad movie from being created. When asked if there is anyone in his life to tell him the product is no good, he answered: "There's a little guy right inside the back [of my head] there saying 'Don't do that.' I don't have a lot of brains but I have a good gut. I'm reasonably intelligent, but I'm certainly not a person who's of high scholastic learning. I feel that what I am today, where I've gone today have been based mostly on instinct."

His instincts were perfect when he became intrigued with a novel by Dennis Lehane called *Mystic River*. The story begins with three childhood friends on the streets of Boston—Jimmy, Sean, and Dave. Young Dave is abducted and abused before finally escaping. Flash forward twenty-five years, and the three still live near each other but are not as close as they used to be. Dave has an ordinary job and continues to struggle with the demons of his past, Jimmy is a former criminal and prisoner, and Sean is a detective. When Jimmy's daughter turns up dead, he vows to find the killer before the police do, and he considers Dave to be one of the prime suspects. Sean has to get to the bottom of the situation before it erupts into something even worse.

After so many disastrous attempts to turn recent popular books into a successful film, Eastwood finally struck gold with *Mystic River*. He did not play a role on-screen but instead focused on producing and directing. He gave the three key roles to well-known actors Sean Penn (Jimmy), Tim Robbins (Dave), and Kevin Bacon (Sean). The public response was overwhelming, and some critics said it was the best directing job of Eastwood's career. At the Academy Awards, Penn and Robbins walked away with Oscars, and the film was nominated for four others, including Best Picture and Best Director. *Mystic River* either won or was nominated for more than a hundred other honors.

"I don't mind telling a dark side," Eastwood said. "Drama usually has some sort of intense conflict. Crimes against children are the most heinous crimes. That, for me, would be a reason for capital punishment because children are innocent and need the guidance of an adult society."

Getting Swank

Hot on the heels of his *Mystic River* success, Eastwood stunned audiences by once again putting out a hit in 2004—and this time it was one of his most powerful films ever. *Million Dollar Baby* tells the story of a boxing trainer named Frankie Dunn, played by Eastwood. Frankie has worked with some of the best fighters in the business, but now, at the end of his career, he is filled with regret. He and his daughter have been estranged for years, and the pain of her absence and of their bad relationship is all but unbearable. Then he meets up with Maggie Fitzgerald—played by Hilary Swank—a penniless waitress from a bad neighborhood who has natural boxing talent and wants to see if she can use it to

Million Dollar Baby earned Clint Eastwood two Academy Awards.

lift herself to a better life. Frankie agrees to train and manage her, obviously in part to fill the void left behind by the absence of his own daughter. What follows is an emotional ride like none other, as Maggie becomes a major force in the ring ... until tragedy strikes.

The reaction from both critics and consumers to *Million Dollar Baby* was immediate and overwhelming. With Eastwood once again producing as well as directing, he managed to shoot the film in just over a month on a budget of only $30 million—and at the box office, it earned well over $200 million, making it one of the most profitable movies of his career. Also notable was the fact that more than half the profits were earned in overseas ticket sales, which underscored the growing importance of foreign distribution and the fact that Eastwood's global popularity was growing.

The critics also loved *Million Dollar Baby*, focusing on the emotional impact of the storyline as well as the magnificent performances of Eastwood, Swank, and Eastwood's longtime friend and seasoned actor Morgan Freeman (who also appeared alongside Eastwood in *Unforgiven*). When the 2004 Academy Awards came around, it was *Million Dollar Baby* that ruled the day, being nominated for seven awards and winning four, including Best Picture, Best Director (Eastwood), Best Actress (Swank), and Best Supporting Actor (Freeman).

Swank was effusive in her praise of Eastwood. "Clint exceeded my expectations and then some. He is obviously very talented. I think this is his best acting to date. He's 74 and it's his best acting I believe. It's in my opinion. I think he's extraordinary in this movie and I think his directing was superb and I was really amazed … But I could literally talk about Clint all day. There's a lot of qualities about him, but some of the ones that really stand out are Clint has a way, he gets people in the movie that he feels are right for the job and his crew. So the people that are surrounding him, he feels are the best people for the job. And then he kind of just says, 'Trust your instinct' and 'don't think too much.' He believes that we have an instinct for a reason and he believes in not thinking too much. But that leads me to the place where he is the most amazing collaborator. He collaborates with everyone, but in the finished product, his fingerprints are all over everything and you didn't even really realize that that was all happening. It's subtle and it's simple and it's really nothing short of astonishing."

Two Sides of the Same War

In 2006, Eastwood directed two films about World War II. The first, *Flags of Our Fathers*, focused on one of the momentous events in American military history: the raising of the American flag during the fierce Battle of Iwo Jima. The central image is iconic—the Pulitzer Prize–winning photo of six soldiers working together to raise an American flag perched atop a pole while they are standing on the peak of a hill. In the film, Eastwood tells of the events leading up to this moment, of the six soldiers involved (five marines and one navy corpsman), and how the event affected their lives.

As always, Eastwood managed to shoot the film in record time—under two months (less than half the time that was planned)—and within budget—$55 million. It was received well by critics, who found the patriotism sincere and effective and Eastwood's direction superb. The film was also nominated for two Academy Awards as well as numerous other honors. However, the public did not warm to it. Box-office sales peaked at about $65 million, just barely making the film profitable.

His other World War II film of 2006 was *Letters from Iwo Jima*. In this instance, he offered viewers the perspective of the Japanese soldiers on Iwo Jima, particularly concerning the tensions between the Japanese general preparing for the forthcoming American invasion and his subordinates, who do not agree with his approach to the battle. Some of the story's content takes the form of letters between soldiers and their loved ones, with the physical letters taking on symbolic meaning at certain points.

CHICK FLICK

Angelina Jolie played a strong woman in *Changeling*.

Eastwood found himself frequently sitting behind the cameras rather than getting in front of them as the new millennium progressed.

In *Changeling*, he returned to the theme of a strong woman he had explored in *Million Dollar Baby*. "I love stories about women," he said in an interview. "I'm not a chick-flick enthusiast but that's what I like about this (*Changeling*). It's a wonderful story of what this woman had to go through and how she has to change and what it does to her life. And that to me is reminiscent of the Forties, of Bette Davis or Joan Crawford or somebody who is trying to overcome something. It seemed like the stories there involved the women more, rather than them just being, you know, fluff. I like that a lot."

Letters from Iwo Jima was meant as a companion piece to *Flags of Our Fathers* and was, in fact, shot at roughly the same time. And although World War II was more than half a century in the past at the time of the release of the films, there was some uncertainty over whether or not American audiences would be receptive to a film that showed their former wartime enemies in a sympathetic light. In fact, *Letters from Iwo Jima* performed much better at the box office, earning a total of nearly $70 million from a budget of under $20 million. It also performed remarkably well in Japan, where it was the number one film for five straight weeks. Critics on both sides of the ocean hailed the work as bold, brave, and sensitive, and Eastwood was praised in particular for portraying the Japanese soldiers as real. *Letters from Iwo Jima* was also recognized with the nomination for and reception of many awards, including four Oscar nominations.

In 2008, he pulled off another significant performance as an actor/director/producer. In *Gran Torino*, Eastwood played Walt Kowalski, a veteran of the Korean War who has recently lost his wife to illness, broken off contact with his extended family, and realized he is living in a neighborhood that has become populated mostly by minorities but had once been filled with white, working-class folks like himself. As a result, he carries around an anger that is gradually consuming him. When Thao, the young son of Walt's next-door neighbors—a Southeast Asian family—tries to steal his beloved Gran Torino as part of a gang initiation, Walt catches him and tells Thao's parents what he's done. Horrified, his parents make the boy work for Walt in order to make amends. Over time, the two come to

Clint Eastwood, shown here in 2012, has continued to produce exceptional films.

respect and even like one another, and when Walt sees Thao heading toward some bad life decisions (that are reminiscent of some of his own mistakes), he takes dramatic steps to save the boy from ending up with the same kind of pain and regret he has carried for so long.

With beautifully performed leads by both Eastwood and his young costar Bee Vang, *Gran Torino* became one of the biggest hits of 2008, starting with a budget of just $33 million and pulling in a staggering $270 million at the box office, plus tens of millions more in DVD sales and rentals. Most critics also hailed the work, finding it an effective commentary on the misfortunes of race relations in America while suggesting a means of improving them.

"In *Gran Torino*, I play a guy who's racially offensive. But he learned. It shows you're never to old to learn and embrace people that you don't understand to begin with," Eastwood said.

Eastwood was also praised for striking a difficult emotional balance within a single character, mixing elements of wit, toughness, and sensitivity to great overall effect.

Now into his eighties, Eastwood has slowed his pace. He does not make as many personal appearances, give as many interviews, or seek as many roles as he once did—yet he is still very much involved in the business and reportedly has interest in continuing to direct and produce. He seems to have a fondness for working with young and established talent, such as Matt Damon (whom he directed in 2009's *Invictus* as well as 2010's *Hereafter*) and Leonardo DiCaprio (the star of the Eastwood-directed and produced *J. Edgar*). What he plans to do beyond that can be nothing more than speculation because he's always done things his way.

"I figure I'm just a guy doing pictures, that's all," he said in an interview. "I'm trying to tell stories and I do the best I can with them and if somebody thinks they're OK, fine, and if somebody doesn't, then that's their opinion and we move on from there."

FILMOGRAPHY

The following is a list of the films Clint Eastwood has directed, written, produced, executive producer, or acted in as of this writing. The films are listed in alphabetical order by year. For a more complete listing, please visit the Internet Movie Database website, www.IMDb.com.

Revenge of the Creature (1955 / actor)

Francis in the Navy (1955 / actor)

Lady Godiva of Coventry (1955 / actor)

Tarantula (1955 / actor)

Never Say Goodbye (1956 / actor)

Star in the Dust (1956 / actor)

Away All Boats (1956 / actor)

The First Traveling Saleslady (1956 / actor)

Escapade in Japan (1957 / actor)

Lafayette Escadrille (1958 / actor)

Ambush at Cimarron Pass (1958 / actor)

A Fistful of Dollars (1964 / actor)

For a Few Dollars More (1965 / actor)

The Good, the Bad and the Ugly (1966 / actor)

The Witches (1966 / actor)

Where Eagles Dare (1968 / actor)

Hang 'em High (1968 / actor)

Coogan's Bluff (1968 / actor)

Paint Your Wagon (1969 / actor, musical score)

Kelly's Heroes (1970 / actor)

Two Mules for Sister Sara (1970 / actor)

The Beguiled (1971 / actor)

Play Misty for Me (1971 / actor, director)

Dirty Harry (1971 / actor)

Joe Kidd (1972 / actor)

High Plains Drifter (1973 / actor, director)

Breezy (1973 / actor, director)

Magnum Force (1973 / actor)

Thunderbolt and Lightfoot (1974 / actor)

The Eiger Sanction (1975 / actor, director)

The Outlaw Josey Wales (1976 / actor, director)

The Enforcer (1976 / actor)

The Gauntlet (1977 / actor, director, musical score)

Every Which Way But Loose (1978 / actor, producer)

Escape from Alcatraz (1979 / actor)

Bronco Billy (1980 / actor, director, musical score)

Any Which Way You Can (1980 / actor, musical score)

Firefox (1982 / actor, director, producer)

Honkytonk Man (1982 / actor, director, producer, musical score)

Sudden Impact (1983 / actor, director, producer)

City Heat (1984 / actor, musical score)

Tightrope (1984 / actor, producer)

Pale Rider (1985 / actor, director, producer)

Heartbreak Ridge (1986 / actor, director, producer, musical score)

The Dead Pool (1988 / actor)

Bird (1988 / director, producer)

Pink Cadillac (1989 / actor)

White Hunter, Black Heart (1990 / actor, director, producer)

The Rookie (1990 / actor, director)

Unforgiven (1992 / actor, director, producer)

In the Line of Fire (1993 / actor)

A Perfect World (1993 / actor, director, musical score)

The Bridges of Madison County (1995 / actor, director, producer, musical score)

The Stars Fell on Henrietta (1995 / producer)

Casper (1995 / actor)

Absolute Power (1997 / actor, director, producer, musical score)

Midnight in the Garden of Good and Evil (1997 / director, producer)

True Crime (1999 / actor, director, producer, musical score)

Space Cowboys (2000 / actor, director, producer)

Blood Work (2002 / actor, director, producer)

Mystic River (2003 / director, producer, musical score)

Million Dollar Baby (2004 / actor, director, producer, musical score)

Flags of Our Fathers (2006 / director, producer, musical score)

Letters from Iwo Jima (2006 / director, producer)

Changeling (2008 / director, producer, musical score)

Gran Torino (2008 / actor, director, producer, musical score)

Invictus (2009 / director, producer)

Hereafter (2010 / director, producer, musical score)

Dave Brubeck: In His Own Sweet Way (2010 / producer)

Kurosawa's Way (2011 / actor)

J. Edgar (2011 / director, producer, musical score)

Trouble with the Curve (2012 / actor, producer)

Jersey Boys (2014 / director)

GLOSSARY

Academy Award—Award of excellence given to a film and/or its cast and crew by the Academy of Motion Picture Arts and Sciences. Also commonly called an "Oscar."

box office—The place where money is collected before people go into a movie theater; gross revenue from ticket sales.

director—The person who oversees the shooting of a movie.

editing—Organizing scenes from a film after it has been shot in order to tell a coherent story.

genre—A category of artistic work, such as comedy, drama, western, sci-fi, etc.

libertarian—A person who believes people should be able to live without interference from the government.

location—A place in the "real world" where a movie is shot, as opposed to a set created in a studio lot and then disassembled afterward.

Oscar—Another name for an Academy Award.

producer—The organizer and general manager of a movie's production.

score—The music written for a movie.

screenwriter—A person who writes the script for a movie.

script—A multipage document outlining the scenes, dialog, emotions, and other details of a movie.

soundstage—A soundproof indoor area where a movie is shot.

BIBLIOGRAPHY

"Clint Eastwood saves life of choking Pebble Beach tournament director." Accessed Feb. 2, 2014. www.washingtonpost.com/blogs/early-lead/wp/2014/02/08/clint-eastwood-saves-life-of-choking-pebble-beach-tournament-director.

Dawson, Jeff, "Dirty Harry Comes Clean." *The Guardian*, June 5, 2008.

Day, Elizabeth, "Gentle man Clint." *The Guardian*, November 2, 2008.

Empire Online, "Clint Eastwood on Clint Eastwood." Accessed Jan. 28, 2014. www.empireonline.com/features/clint-eastwood-on-clint-eastwood/default.asp.

Hainey, Michael, "Icon: Clint Eastwood." *GQ*, December 2009.

Harris, Mark, "The Leo Tapes." *GQ*, September 2011.

Hughes, Howard, *Aim for the Heart: The Films of Clint Eastwood*. New York, NY, I.B. Taurus, 2009.

Macklin, Tony, "Plant Your Feet and Tell the Truth: An Interview with Clint Eastwood," *Bright Lights Film Journal*, February 2005.

McGilligan, Patrick, *Clint: The Life and Legend*, New York, NY, HarperCollins, 1999.

Miller, Paul, "Eastwood and his big family mourn their matriarch." *The Carmel Pine Cone*, February 10, 2006.

MovieWeb Team, "Hilary Swank talks 'Million Dollar Baby.'" January 2005. Accessed on Jan. 30, 2014. www.movieweb.com/news/hilary-swank-talks-million-dollar-baby.

O'Keefe, Eric, "Clint Eastwood Goes One on One with The Land Report." *The Land Report*, November 2007.

Walters, Barbara. "Barbara Walters Special with Clint Eastwood." YouTube Video, posted April 27, 2013. www.youtube.com/watch?v=SZHc3zmtYdw

SOURCE NOTES

Chapter 1

Pg. 4: *Pink Cadillac*, Warner Bros., 1989.

Pgs. 6–7: Walters, Barbara, "Barbara Walters Special with Clint Eastwood," www.youtube.com/watch?v=SZHc3zmtYdw.

Pgs. 7–8: Day, Elizabeth, "Gentle man Clint", *The Guardian*, November 2, 2008.

Pg. 8: Miller, Paul, "Eastwood and his big family mourn their matriarch."

Pg. 14: Harris, Mark, "The Leo Tapes", *GQ*, December 2009.

Chapter 2

Pg. 18: McGilligan, Patrick, *Clint: The Life and Legend*, (New York: HarperCollins, 1999), p. 94.

Pg. 20: Hughes, Howard, *Aim for the Heart: The Films of Clint Eastwood*, (New York: I.B. Taurus, 2009)

Pg. 21: Dawson, Jeff, "Dirty Harry Comes Clean," www.theguardian.com/film/2008/jun/06/1.

Pg. 22: Walters, "Barbara Walters Special with Clint Eastwood."

Pg. 26: Walters, "Barbara Walters Special with Clint Eastwood."

Pg. 26: Empire Online, "Clint Eastwood on Clint Eastwood", www.empireonline.com/features/clint-eastwood-on-clint-eastwood/default.asp.

Pg. 27: Dawson, Jeff, "Dirty Harry Comes Clean," www.theguardian.com/film/2008/jun/06/1.

Chapter 3

Pgs. 28, 30: O'Keefe, Eric, "Clint Eastwood Goes One on One with The Land Report," *The Land Report*, November 2007.

Pg. 31: Walters, "Barbara Walters Special with Clint Eastwood."

Pg. 31: Miller, "Eastwood and his big family mourn their matriarch."

Pg. 33: O'Keefe, Eric, "Clint Eastwood Goes One on One with The Land Report."

Pg. 33: *Washington Post*, "Clint Eastwood saves life of choking Pebble Beach tournament director," www.washingtonpost.com/blogs/early-lead/wp/2014/02/08/clint-eastwood-saves-life-of-choking-pebble-beach-tournament-director.

Pg. 33: *Washington Post*, "Clint Eastwood saves life of choking Pebble Beach tournament director."

Chapter 4

Pg. 36: Hainey, Michael, "Icon: Clint Eastwood," www.gq.com/entertainment/men-of-the-year/2009/badass/clint-eastwood-legend-invictus-director.

Pg. 37: Empire Online, "Clint Eastwood on Clint Eastwood," www.empireonline.com/features/clint-eastwood-on-clint-eastwood/default.asp.

Pg. 37: Empire Online, "Clint Eastwood on Clint Eastwood."

Pg. 38: Day, "Gentle Man Clint."

Pgs. 43–44: Macklin, Tony, "Plant Your Feet and Tell the Truth: An Interview with Clint Eastwood", brightlightsfilm.com/47/clint.php#.UzsgMqXqKhM.

Chapter 5

Pg. 50: Harris, "The Leo Tapes."

Pg. 53: Macklin, "Plant Your Feet and Tell the Truth: An Interview with Clint Eastwood."

Pg. 56: Walters, "Barbara Walters Special with Clint Eastwood."

Pg. 58: MovieWeb Team, "Hilary Swank talks 'Million Dollar Baby,'" www.movieweb.com/news/hilary-swank-talks-million-dollar-baby.

Pg. 60: Day, "Gentle man Clint."

Pg. 63: Hainey, "Icon: Clint Eastwood."

Pg. 63: Day, "Gentle man Clint."

FURTHER INFORMATION

Books

Garza, Sarah. *Action! Making Movies*. Huntington Beach, CA: Teacher Created Materials, 2013.

Hermansson, Casie. *How to Analyze the Films of Clint Eastwood*. Minneapolis, MN: Essential Library, 2012.

Kapsis, Robert E., and Kathie Coblentz. *Clint Eastwood (Conversations with Filmmakers)*. Jackson, MS: University Press of Mississippi, 2012.

Schickel, Richard. *Clint Eastwood: A Biography*. New York, NY: Vintage, 2011.

Schickel, Richard, and Clint Eastwood. *Clint: A Retrospective*. New York, NY: Sterling, 2010.

Websites

IMDB Clint Eastwood page

www.imdb.com/name/nm0000142

Plenty of Eastwood-related info on the most comprehensive movie-industry data site on the Web.

Box Office Mojo: Clint Eastwood

www.boxofficemojo.com/people/
chart/?id=clinteastwood.htm

All the information you'll ever need about the sales figures of Eastwood's films, as well as which studio distributed them, release dates, and more.

Clint Eastwood Tribute Page

www.clinteastwood.net

Possibly the best of all the Clint Eastwood fan sites, it features an extensive collection of multimedia items, including audio clips, video clips, photographs, and more.

INDEX

Page numbers
in **boldface** are
illustrations

Malpaso Productions,
52
Maslin, Janet, 39–40

National Film
Preservation Board
of the Library of
Congress, 38
National Film Registry,
38

Pebble Beach National
Pro-Am, 33

Reeves, Jacelyn Allen,
41
Republican National
Convention, 4
Ruiz, Dina Maria, 12

Siegel, Don, 26, 34, **35**,
38, 42
Spaghetti westerns,
18–19, 21, 37
Sparks, Robert, 16
Streep, Meryl, 45–46
Swank, Hilary, 56, 58

Tehama, 11, 28, 30,
31–32
Tehama Golf Club, 33

Universal Studios, 14

Waller, Robert James,
44
Walters, Barbara, 6, 26
Warner Brothers, 40, 42
Wood, Margaret Ruth
Eastwood (Ruth), 6,
8, 31–32
World War I, 6
World War II, 8, 59, 61

ABOUT THE AUTHOR

Wil Mara has been an ardent fan of Clint Eastwood since he was dragged kicking and screaming to an afternoon matinee of *High Plains Drifter* in the summer of 1973. He has written many books for the school library market, including three other titles in Cavendish Square's Great Filmmakers series. More information about his work can be found at www.wilmara.com.